YO-DBU-073

# when *someone* **you** know is *sexually* abused

by susie shellenberger

PUBLISHING

COLORADO SPRINGS, COLORADO

**Library of Congress Cataloging-in-Publication Data**
Shellenberger, Susie
When someone you know is sexually abused / Susie Shellenberger
    p.  cm. — (Let's talk about life ; 3)
Summary: Uses a variety of literary forms to address the facts and
feelings surrounding sexual abuse, focusing mainly on incest and
directed particularly at the teenage girl.
   ISBN 1-56179-448-1
    1. Incest victims—Psychology—Juvenile literature. 2. Sexually
abused teenagers—Psychology—Juvenile literature. 3. Child sexual
abuse—Psychological aspects—Juvenile literature. 4. Child sexual
abuse—Religious aspects—Christianity—Juvenile literature.
[1. Incest. 2. Child sexual abuse.] I. Title. II. Series.
HV6570.6.S54 1996
362.7'6—dc20
                        95–49796
                            CIP
                            AC

Published by Focus on the Family Publishing, Colorado Springs,
Colorado 80995. Distributed in the U.S.A. and Canada by Word
Books, Dallas, Texas.

Cover Design: The Puckett Group

Printed in the United States of America

96 97 98 99 00/10 9 8 7 6 5 4 3 2

# About This Book

*A*s a youth minister for seven years, a schoolteacher for four years, and now a teen magazine editor, I care about teens. I enjoy laughing with them, sharing Cokes and pizzas, and hearing their struggles. Oftentimes, caring about teens means crying and praying with them.

*Brio* magazine, the publication I edit, receives about 1,000 letters every month from teen girls all over the world. Each letter that contains a return address is answered by a staff who loves teens. Many times our hearts break with the pain we read on the pages.

Because sexual abuse is such a widespread problem—one that shows up often in the letters we receive—we thought we might be able to offer some hope and help to the many girls who have written . . . and to the girls who are too frightened to even pick up a pen.

We've chosen to focus mainly on one area of sexual abuse—incest. Much of what you'll read on these pages, though, will also apply to someone who has experienced *any* kind of sexual abuse. Let me explain how this book works.

**Part I** will help you understand and identify the emotions of a friend who's being sexually abused. The first poem, "What I'm Feeling," was written from the perspective of a victim. The poem "Sharing the Pain" was written from my experience as a youth minister trying to help a member of my youth group through her struggles. Incest can happen to anyone. It's not selective of age, race, or status. Incest victims can live in wealthy or impoverished neighborhoods and can come from Christian or non-Christian homes.

As you read "Sharing the Pain," notice that an incest victim often vacillates between emotions—grateful for help and intervention one week and angry at knowledge of her secret and outside involvement the next week. This is a common trait of sexually abused kids. They want help, but they don't want disclosure. If you're trying to help a friend who's a victim of incest, don't get your feelings hurt if she ignores you one day and wants to be your best friend the next. Stick with her—no matter what.

**Part II** deals with facts and information about incest. If you or someone you know is trapped in an incestuous situation, this information will help you deal with the problem.

**Part III** showcases two fiction stories that will help you understand how widespread this problem can be. Incest can happen within an immediate family or with extended family members. Though this book places the spotlight mainly on incest, the second fiction story will highlight a girl who's being sexually abused by someone *outside* her family.

**Part IV** shows the hope that incest victims can cling to when they allow God to take control of the pain. Jill, a real-life victim, shares how she lived through the nightmare to experience God's healing. There's a path of wholeness for *all* victims . . . if they choose it.

Everyone who helped put this book together wants you to know that we care about you. **You may be trapped in an incestuous home.** It's my prayer that through this book—and with God's help—you'll move from being a victim to becoming a survivor.

**You may have a friend who's being sexually abused.** My prayer is that you'll stand behind her, pray *for* her and *with* her, and lead her to a trusted adult with whom she can share her trauma and begin the healing process.

*Part I*

# The Heart
# of a Victim

## What I'm Feeling

They tell us quite often
how to protect ourselves
when on the street
or when out after dark . . .

But why doesn't anyone tell us
how to protect ourselves after dark
in our own homes?

And sometimes
even when all the lights are still on?

Today
instead of doing our times threes

the teacher said we would have a special lesson.

It was about safety and stuff.
She told us what to do
if anyone abused our bodies.

"Tell your parents," the teacher said.

So I told Mommy.
She yelled and said I was bad.
Then she sent me to bed without any supper.

*Why did I tell?*

Now,
tonight
when he comes home,
it will hurt worse than ever . . .

I'm so scared.
And Teacher . . .
*you were wrong.*

◦──◦

It was the middle of September.
Dad came home early.
The school bus had barely dropped me off
and I had invited Julie over to play hopscotch.
Dad told me to come inside . . .
said he had come home early just to be with me.

My stomach tensed.
My legs began to shake.
I begged to finish playing hopscotch with Julie.
We had just started.
Dad sent her home.

When I still refused,
he grabbed my arm
and jerked my whole body off the ground
and into the house.

It hurt.
I screamed.
Julie ran.

Dad was so strong.
I was so small—
and frightened.
He always got his way.

. . . and Julie never came back.

It's happening again.
The lights are out and
Mommy sent me to bed hours ago.
She told me to sleep tight
so I would remember how to write all the words
on the spelling test tomorrow.

But I can't go to sleep.
I'm scared.
My face is all wet and sticky from tears.
Your rough hands are hurting me.

I will hold my teddy bear a little closer—
clutch him a little tighter
. . . and once again
pretend I am at Amy's house
and we are having tea
with her new dishes.

It wasn't until the eighth grade
that I realized what was going on
between us was not normal.

I had always hated it.
And it always made me physically sick.
But you said every family was like this.
And because "parents are always right,"
I believed you.

Then came Friday.
Traci and I spent the night at her house
so we could work on our book reports together.
My report was on journalism.
Hers was on something called incest.

I'd never heard of it before.

She let me thumb through the book.
So that's what they call it.
I didn't even know there was a name
for what you had forced me to do.

I asked Traci if it was wrong.
She said it was.
Said people could go to jail for it.
I gave the book back—
afraid to read the words
for fear of my name being
       somewhere on the pages.

Then I ran into the bathroom and threw up.

Today in biology class
we saw the sex education films
and had open discussion afterward.

All the other kids listened intently
interrupting only occasionally
with nervous giggles.

I tried to pretend
that I was as interested as everyone else.
But the subject was not new to me.
My firsthand experience
went a lot further
than the chapter we were studying.

I got physically ill
and was sent to the nurse's office.
She said it was probably the flu.
I knew better.

*What would it feel like,* I wondered,
*to simply be a student . . . and not a victim?*

Just once
I'd like to be hugged by you
the way Jamie's dad hugs her.

Just once
I'd like to sit next to you
and not have to worry about your hands.

Just once
I'd like to live a day in my own home
without being terrified.

Just once
I'd like to know that
when I shut the door
to my bedroom
or the bathroom,
it would stay shut.

Just once . . .
I'd like my wishes to come true.

## Sharing the Pain

*I* took 48 high school teenagers on tour.
After our successful evening performance
they were too excited to call it a night.

Their spontaneity turned the hotel parking
lot into a Broadway stage. Creative energy
personified itself in the midnight Houston
humidity. Rhythm from portable stereos
became live motion.

Nearby, gymnastics into the deep end of the
midsized pool exploded like fireworks.

I expected your laughter and talent to permeate

the after-hours celebration. Instead, you sat
alone . . . tears glistening against the moonlight.

I strained to distinguish your soft words
against the electrified tones just meters away.

Like bread torn in communion, you broke each
word and gave it away in desperation.

"Things at home.
It's my dad.
*He . . .* "

My energy turned to anger.
Fireworks **burned** inside.
I enforced a curfew. The music stopped.
Completely.

The parking lot empty, I returned to you—
a 16-year-old child-adult sitting alone on the curb
outside the Holiday Inn in Houston, Texas.

I was naive. Didn't know *anything* about incest.
But I *did* know the Shepherd always headed for
the hurting sheep. So I held you in my arms and
rocked you . . . as if motion could somehow
comfort the pain.
We cried for two and a half hours.

The remainder of the tour brought great reviews.

But the rhythm was never the same.
The music died with Joanie—
the 16-year-old child-adult.

⌒

Susie,
I'm sitting here in my room,
with the teddy bear on one side
and a box of Kleenex on the other.

Parents are asleep.
Billy's tucked in.
Tim's on the phone.

My mind drifts back to those few weeks
I stayed with you after we returned
        from the tour.
You ironed my clothes when I was running late,
hugged me
and got me off to work on time.

When I'd come in from cheerleading practice—
and you from a meeting with someone in our
        youth group—
we'd grab something to eat
and just talk.
Sometimes we'd cry.

I loved the nights you came in with your guitar,
sat on the edge of my bed and sang.

That always seemed to calm my nerves.
So many times I told you to go away.
I'm glad you didn't.

When you finally put your guitar away
and headed off to bed,
my heart was screaming, "No! Don't leave me."

Thanks for giving me your home when
    I needed it.
Though the pain never left,
you gave me hope.

Joanie,
I'm worried about you.
You never eat.
You average two hours of sleep each night.
You work a part-time job,
and somehow you manage to stay involved
in school and church activities.

What's going to happen to you?
When will your breaking point come?
Someday will you just explode from all
    the pressure inside?

You work harder than anyone I know
to make everyone else believe your world
    is normal.

The class-favorite personality.
The cheerleader.
No one even suspects that you're breaking
        on the inside.

I'm worried about you.
You're becoming too good at acting.

～

God,
**Why do You have to be our *Father*?**
**That name makes it so hard to trust You,**
**believe You**
**and even *want* to love You.**

**Susie told me not to think of You as a man**
**but as some kind of spiritual being . . .**
**our Creator and Sustainer—**
**Someone who loves me more than I can**
            **imagine.**
**Someone who wants to take care of me forever.**

**But when I pray, I see Jesus.**
**I know the Bible says He is pure and godly,**
                **without sin,**
                **a miracle-worker.**

**But just when my prayers start to get through,**
**I remember that behind that white robe is the**
**body of a *man*.**

God,
help me!

⌒—◦

Susie,
You're probably wondering why I'm not
    at church tonight.
I didn't come . . . because I'm angry.

You always told me that if I said
"I don't want to talk about it," I wouldn't
    have to.
You always said that my body and the details
    of my life
were *my* choice to share or to keep.

Well,
yesterday when you took me to the doctor,
    I said that.
Three times!
She asked so many questions and didn't
    back down
when I said I didn't want to answer.

So I just gave short yes-no answers.
But by the end of the appointment,
she ended up knowing so much more
    than I intended.

Don't you understand

14

how *important* it is to me not to tell anybody?
It tears me up inside.

She wants me back in one week, so she can
    ask more questions.
Please understand why I can't go.
I *won't*.

        ⌐⌐⌐○

God,
In my office once again . . . planning retreats
and choir tours and the big discipleship kickoff
    next week.
My mind is drifting. . . .

I catch myself glancing at my watch
and trying to remember what class Joanie's in.
Picturing locker #320
and her stack of books all mixed together.
Central High School. Her world.

*Home ec:* Trying to visualize how far along her
dress is by now and how the material we picked
out looks.

*World literature:* She called last night around 2:30
A.M. Said she couldn't sleep because of the nightmares. Isn't ready for the book report that's due
today. Wondering if she'll be called on to report.

*Trig:* Supposed to have a test today. More tension to add to her already pressure-filled world.

*Health:* Wondering if the open discussion is still on abuse, and if I'll be getting a phone call in a minute relaying the aloneness.

I want to intercede, Father.
Teach me how to help carry the weight.
When there are no more tears left for her to cry,
let them fill *my* eyes.

When she can't find the words, let *me* seek them.

When she has no strength,
allow *me* to stand in her place.

Show me how to make intercession
*a living reality.*

⌒⌒

**Susie,**
**It's 11 P.M.**
**Company and family are all in bed.**
**I'm sitting here in the living room**
**watching the lights on the Christmas tree blink**
**on and off.**

**Is it okay to say "I'm hurting"?**

A couple of weeks ago, my counselor said,
"Don't deny your feelings. Let yourself feel."

But I'm scared to.
I feel like a little girl inside screaming,
"If I do, will you still love me?
Will you accept me when I look silly
with black mascara running down my face
and I can't talk because of the lump
        in my throat?"

I hurt so bad inside.
I'm so scared.
I'm all confused.

Will I ever be normal?

Susie,
You promised that you'd never make decisions
about my life . . . without me.
I begged . . .
but you wouldn't give in.
Now, months later, I am in another home
with another family.

What have I done?
Only bad kids are sent away.

Isn't it sad?

**You've destroyed the very thing in me
that you tried to rescue me from . . .
my freedom to make choices.**

~

Joanie,
Maybe someday you'll understand
why I had to involve other people.
Then again . . . maybe you'll *never* understand.

I realize I'm taking the risk of you turning
on me forever.
But can't you see that my concern for you
goes way beyond how you feel toward *me?*

Your friendship is important to me.
But your emotional survival is *more important.*
I care whether you like or hate me—
but I care *more* about you grabbing hold
of all the promise and potential wrapped
within your future.
Ambivalence.
Love me. Hate me. Cry on my shoulder.
Scream and walk away.
It doesn't change the *fact* that I'm committed
to helping you.
I will wait this thing out.
I'll continue to walk by your side . . .
even when you're angry.

~

Susie,
Why do you do it?
Over and over and over again,
through a calm voice and reassurance,
you pull out of me
my painful memories until I'm drowning
     in them.

For a while you feel them, too—
the hurt and the confusion.
But then you can forget and go home.

I CAN'T!

Once again you've left me—
hurting.

       ⟳

Susie,
Looking back over the last six months . . .
you've been so positive and reassuring.
I appreciate you.
Thanks for always going that extra mile.

       ⟳

Susie,
Sometimes I wonder if I am *his* victim
     or *yours*. . . .

Victim to the manipulative way

you talk me into doing things I later regret—
for a lifetime.

Like talking with a social worker.
Like changing my home life forever.

I'm feeling so desperate to get away from you.
But because of the security you give that I need,
I won't.
This time.

Joanie,
Did you think I would merely listen and
        then forget?
Someone who would only wipe the tears away
for the time being and then send you on your way
with the empty promise of "things will get better"?

I *had* to do something.
How could I have lived with myself—
or even slept at night—
knowing that you were trapped in an
        inescapable prison?

Even *you* admitted to me
that you could not survive emotionally
one more year in your situation.

I know I said I would never tell anyone.

I made a rash promise in desperation to
     comfort you.
It was an initial reaction made at midnight
     on tour.

I had no right to make a promise so bold.
I had no idea of the consequences or
how tightly you were bound.

I quickly and impulsively made a promise
     I knew nothing about.

Will you forgive me?
I am so sorry, Joanie.
Not for breaking the promise—
but for making a promise I couldn't keep.

       ⌁

**Susie,**
**I can't describe how bad I feel**
**about the things I said to you last week.**
**So here I am—on my 15-minute break—**
     **with a Diet Coke, crying.**
**I am so sorry.**

**I feel guilty inside. And angry. And sad.**
**I feel like I'm being destroyed by emotions**
     **that are out of control.**
**Please stop this volcano.**
**I'm afraid I'm losing the battle.**

Joanie,
We were walking out of the judge's office.
You said nothing until we got to the car.
You turned to me with a look on your face
     that's frozen in my mind.

With a shaking voice you relayed what
     the judge had told you.

"She said that she wanted to put me in a home
situation where I would feel secure. Safe. A place
where I wouldn't have to worry about anything
else except what I would decide to wear to
school the next day!"

Your eyes filled with disbelief,
and for the first time since I've known you,
I saw genuine hope stretch across your face.
It was as if the realization that "things really
don't have to be this way" had finally penetrated
your thinking.

Then you looked at me with wonder.
"Susie, is that what other kids worry about?
What they'll wear to school?"

My heart splintered once again.
I wanted to hold you like a child,

wipe your tears and somehow remove the
      tremendous burden
you carried.

We started home.
You leaned against the car door and shut
      your eyes.
I stared at the road—my thoughts mixing
      with the traffic . . .
*It's ironic. Most kids fight to be adults.*
*But you have to fight for the right **just to be a kid.***

      ⌒

Susie,
I've made progress this year because of you.
I'm glad God gave you to me.
But sometimes I still take steps backward.
For years, secrecy had become a way of
      life for me.
And even though we've made progress,
I want to run away from it all.
I want to hide.

Sometimes I think there is very little
that stands between me and insanity.
I feel bad if I tell. I feel bad if I don't.
I'm falling apart on the inside.

I can't seem to grab hold of the fact that
      I'm really worth something.

I wish security was an object—something
     I could buy
and hang on to. Instead, it's something I have
     to work for.
Most of the time I feel like I don't even
     deserve to be secure.

How do I get over the self-hate?
It's not really *me* I hate. It's my body and
     what it can do.
Do you understand?

My past haunts me.
And I'm curious . . .
will it ever leave me alone?

Joanie,
A year ago, you dared to take the biggest risk
     in your life.
Sitting on a curb outside a hotel,
you chose to break the silence that had robbed
     you of childhood—
the trauma that had made you a prisoner in
     your own home.

Soon afterward came the pain of separation and
the continual gnawing of fear—wondering if
you'd done the right thing by sharing such an
enormous secret.

But also came the opportunity to see the real
        YOU—
a terrific young lady discovering God's direction
        in her life,
fully capable of making her own decisions—
and the realization that you deserve to add
        the phrases
"I need" and "I want" to your vocabulary.

I have never been naive enough to pretend
        I understand.
I've never said, "I know what you're going
        through."
I don't.
Only you have the power to try to help me
        see inside.
I wish we could pretend that your past is simply
        a nightmare
that will fade after the morning has come
        and gone.
But this isn't just a bad dream, is it?

To say it's been a hard year is much more than
        an understatement.
You've been under another roof—lived with
        a different family—
left everything familiar, the only home you
        ever knew.

It was a matter of safety.

A question of emotional survival.
The desire for you to regain the control of
        your body
that was taken from you so long ago.
The need for you to realize that *you* are in
        control of *you*.
That you have the right to set limits and draw
        boundaries.
The necessity to know what is normal and
        what isn't.
And the need for you to be able to sleep at night
without the fear of being intruded upon.

This year brought many changes.
A new home. Counseling. Strained friendships.
        The fear of insanity.

But we have walked *together*.
We have shared tears, lunches, prayers,
        sunburns, and giggles.
We have talked into the wee hours of the
morning, made funnel cakes, tuna melts,
        and solid memories.

When you told me your secret, I made an agape
        commitment to you—
a commitment of walking *with* you through
the painful healing process, and a commitment
to keep you before our heavenly Father in
consistent prayer.

You see, Joanie, when we base our security in a *relationship* with Jesus Christ, He sets us free to love others. He causes us to invest our lives into helping those around us draw closer to Him. He directs our time and energies into making a life-time difference for someone.

Someday, you too will invest your life into patching up the broken heart of another. And you'll do it not because it's part of your job, but because of your growing relationship with the Lord.

As He changes *your* life, you'll help change
    someone else's.
God dreams BIG dreams for you, Joanie.
I can't wait to hear from you . . . 10 years
    from now.

*Part II*

*Facts*

We've all heard how important it is to obey our parents. And for most children, that means keeping their rooms clean, doing their homework, and coming home on time. For the child who is from a dysfunctional or troubled home, however, obeying his or her parents can mean being abused.

Studies suggest that one out of every four girls is sexually abused by someone in her family. For boys, the figure is one out of seven. With numbers this high—and these are *reported* cases only—it's likely that someone in your class at school or in your church youth group is trapped in a sexually abusive situation.

# What Is It?

Sexual activity among family members is called incest, and it's the most common type of sexual abuse. Incest comes from the Greek word *cestus*, meaning pure. Putting the "in" before it forms the word *impure*. Incest not only happens within *immediate* families but in *extended* families as well (stepparents, grandparents, uncles, stepbrothers, and so on).

Incest may be covert (concealed or less obvious) or overt (out in the open or blatant—something physical between two people). Jodie's uncle committed covert incest when he forced her to look at pornographic magazines. Ann's stepbrother committed covert incest when he took photos of her undressing. Rachel experienced overt incest when she was alone with her grandfather and he began touching her sexual organs.

It doesn't matter whether incest is covert or overt, it's still sexual abuse and is always a *crime*. Incest has been reported in every race of people in every era of time. If you're a victim of incest, you are *not* alone. (And neither are you at fault; but we'll talk more about that later, okay?)

The seven types of incest in order of prevalence are:

1. Daughter/father (or stepfather)
2. Daughter/another adult family member (uncle, grandfather, etc.)
3. Brother/sister

4. Father/son
5. Son/adult male family member
6. Mother/son
7. Mother/daughter

Incest most frequently begins occurring between the ages of 8 and 13, but some children are victims much younger. If you've experienced incest, you may have a hard time knowing what kind of affection within a family is normal. Hugging, kissing, patting each other on the back, and even playful wrestling or tickling are all normal. But if a family member touches you in a private area, insists that you touch him or her in a private area, or French-kisses you (tongue kissing), that is NOT normal and is considered incestuous. Also, as mentioned earlier, some abuse involves things not so straightforward, such as pornography or sexually oriented games or activities.

# Characteristics of an Incestuous Family

Although specific traits of abusive families may vary, researchers and mental-health workers have identified some typical patterns:

• *The parents had little love expressed to them as children and may have been victims themselves.* Therefore, they may have trouble seeing family life as anything different from an abusive situation. Frequently, abuse is passed on from generation to generation unless someone decides to change the pattern.

- *The family denies that incest is happening.*
Many times, a parent is so shocked to discover
that the child has been molested by a family
member that he or she refuses to believe it. It's
easier to pretend that the problem will go away if
it's not talked about. For parents who were
abused themselves, it's especially easy to deny
that abuse is happening again, because they
didn't know how to deal with it *then,* and they
don't want to deal with it *now.*

- *The family operates on a closed system of communication, which means little about its activities and
rules are discussed outside the family.* Oftentimes,
communication *within* the family is poor as well.
Things just aren't talked about. The message com-
municated, either subtly or clearly, is, "We don't
comment about the family rules, and we don't get
our needs met outside of the family."

- *The child is forced to assume an adult role.*
For instance, if the mother is severely ill or absent
from the family, the daughter will assume the
motherly duties of cooking, cleaning, and other
household responsibilities. An abusive father
then may pull her into a sexual role as well.

- *The family doesn't react typically to things.*
Emotions may be volatile, changing quickly and
without warning. A parent may overreact to a
common event. For example, a father who is
sexually abusing a daughter may become

extremely angry or jealous at her attempt to have male friends.

• *A role reversal takes place.* The child becomes the parent, and the parent gets taken care of. This sometimes happens in alcoholic homes, when the parent becomes irresponsible and undependable, so the child becomes the responsible, reliable one. In a sense, she takes on the role of parent.

• *Communication among family members is filled with rage or is even violent.* An abusive family doesn't know how to calmly disagree with one another and express differences rationally. If a child disagrees with the parent, a common reaction would be anger instead of an open-minded exchange of ideas and feelings.

• *Sexuality and aggression are fused together.* Sex isn't seen as an act of love and commitment to a lifetime partner; it's seen as a display of power and sometimes even punishment.

## Characteristics of an Abuser

• *He usually shifts the blame to the girl or the mother.* ("Your mom is too busy to meet my needs." Or, "If your mom was the kind of wife she *should* be, I wouldn't have to turn to *you* for sexual fulfillment." Or, "You ask for it by the way you dress and act.")

• *He has mastered the system of denial and regularly rationalizes his behavior.* ("It's okay that we're doing this, but you have to understand that it's *our* little secret." Or, "I'm just teaching you about sex so you'll know what's going on in the real world.")

  • *He uses his children to bolster his sense of power and to receive comfort.* Parental or adult authority is used to push his kids into meeting his sexual needs.

  • *He can be highly religious or moralistic.* Some abusers are members of their local church and appear "perfect" on the outside.

  • *He may have been a victim himself.* Since he was abused, he uses this history as a guide for how he treats his own children.

## What About the Mothers?

Mothers who live in an incestuous environment are often:

  • overly submissive and incapable of protecting themselves and their children.
  • physically ill or away from home much of the time.
  • feeling trapped in the marriage.
  • experiencing a high degree of stress (because the incestuous family rarely seeks help for its problems).

## Reaching Out to a Friend

It's likely that one of your friends at school or in your church youth group is trapped in an incestuous environment. If you suspect a friend is being sexually abused, look for these signs:

- Low self-esteem
- Difficulty in establishing proper relationships with the opposite sex (either completely withdrawn or promiscuous)
- Self-mutilation (cutting or burning herself)
- Reacts in a defensive manner when touched
- Dramatic changes in school performance
- Complains of frequent "general" pains
- Mood swings (happy one minute, sad the next)
- Severe depression
- Eating problems (Sexual abuse can lead to eating disorders, such as anorexia nervosa or bulimia. In fact, some researchers say that 80 percent of all eating disorders can be traced to sexual abuse.)
- Extreme hostility toward parents
- Overreacting to common problems
- Fearful of basements, closets, or dark spaces
- Feeling unworthy of God's love and forgiveness
- Displaced anger (She's angry but directs her anger at the wrong person—maybe *you!*)

Though some of the above characteristics can result from other problems, if you notice that a friend displays *several* of them, it may be a sign that she's being sexually abused.

If you think one of your friends is being abused, it's time to consider sharing your suspicions with a trusted adult. But don't act *too* quickly—nobody likes rumors and misinformation about them spread around. In fact, the reputations of honest and totally innocent parents and families have been ruined because of false rumors and gossip.

Get the facts first. Gently approach your friend and ask a few leading questions. Let her know that you can be trusted. Remind her how much you care about her and value her friendship. She may not share her problem right away, but the important thing is that you stand by her—especially when she's angry or depressed.

## Breaking the Silence

When your friend *does* decide to talk about her sexual abuse, realize that there's an immediate crisis the moment she tells you! Because you are now aware of the situation, things can never be the same again. By consciously choosing to share such a painful, personal part of her life with you, she is also choosing to break the conspiracy of silence.

It's important to realize that your friend has

spent a long time building and maintaining a silent wall around this private area of her life. This intimate secret has been meticulously guarded. She will be very nervous about what you might do with this new information, so be extremely careful about how you proceed!

Try to express your concern in the following ways:

**1. Thank her for sharing her secret with you.** Gently explain that you're not equipped to handle such a huge problem, but that you'll help her in any way you can.

**2. Pray with her.** Remind her that God feels her pain. Memorize this verse together: "The Lord is close to those whose hearts are breaking" (Psalm 34:18 TLB).

**3. Cry with her.** If you genuinely feel like crying, there's no need to hold back. Sometimes tears say a lot more than words. Let her know that you share her pain.

**4. Listen, listen, listen.** The healing process begins when the secret is revealed, and your friend may want to talk about her experiences and her pain. If so, practice good listening skills—focus your entire attention on her, don't interrupt, maintain eye contact. If your friend isn't comfortable opening up, don't push or pry. She'll talk when she's ready.

**5. Help her sort through the confusion, but don't give advice.** Your friend will probably be confused about A LOT of things—her parents, her faith, her values, and her feelings. For a while, she may feel that everything in her world is chaotic. YOU can be the one stable thing in her life, the one who points her to the Stabilizer Himself, Jesus Christ. Still, be careful not to give unasked-for advice. Your job is to be a friend, not to try to fix everything.

**6. Don't walk out on her.** You may feel uncomfortable receiving such intimate and personal information. You might be embarrassed and nervous. That's all right—it's perfectly normal to feel that way. Whatever you do, though, don't ignore or avoid your friend or her problem. That would break her trust at the very time she needs it most.

For your friend, the hard stuff is just beginning. Remembering (or sharing) an abusive situation is like a puzzle falling into place *one piece at a time.* As the experiences and emotions come together, she'll need a tremendous amount of support! Plan on being involved in her life the next several months or years.

**7. Point her toward qualified professionals.** She may feel as though her whole life is a puzzle—but she'll also begin to realize that one important piece is missing. That piece is her childhood. She was robbed of a normal, healthy childhood. Like all of us who lose something important, she needs to grieve the loss. This means she needs a professional counselor to guide her through this process.

YOU are not equipped to help put her life back together. If you're a true friend, you'll help her find the right people to talk to.

**8. Don't make promises you can't keep.** In trying to comfort and console your friend, you may be tempted to make promises you won't be able to live up to. Do NOT promise that you won't tell anyone. If her situation is to ever get better, you HAVE to tell someone eventually! This is *not* a secret for two teens to keep between themselves. A trusted adult *must* be brought into the situation or your friend will never get the help she needs and deserves.

Before your friend even shares her problem with you, she might say, "I need to tell you something, but you have to promise you'll never tell anyone!" This should immediately clue you in to how frightened she is. Don't make that promise because you're curious and want to know what's bugging her. And don't make that promise because you feel sorry for her. A good response would be: "I care about you very much, and I want to help. I can tell something's bothering you, and it must be pretty important for you to want me to make such a bold promise. But *because* I care, I can't make that promise. I will, however, promise to stand by you. THAT you can count on."

**9. Be honest.** While you don't want to make rash promises that you can't keep, you *do* want to offer honest comfort. Here are a few things you CAN say *after* she has shared her situation with you:

"Because I care about you, I cannot let you continue to be abused."

"Together, we need to decide how to get you the help you need."

"I will have to intervene."

"I am not trained or qualified to handle this situation by myself. I need your permission to involve another person."

**10. Be there.** Your presence is far more important than having the right words to say or knowing exactly what to do. Sometimes there *aren't* any words that will comfort. Don't feel like you have to say just the right thing. Simply *be* with her. Be willing to sit right next to her in total silence for a couple of hours if that's what she needs. Your presence will speak volumes to your frightened, lonely friend.

## If You've Experienced Incest

If *you* are a victim of abuse, you may have been told—by the abuser—that this incestuous situation is your fault. You may have been persuaded that you've even done something to encourage the abuse. DON'T BELIEVE IT FOR A SECOND! And if you're feeling any guilt at all, it's false guilt. You are not to blame.

*No adult EVER has the right to be sexually suggestive or sexually intimate with a child or teenager (or even a nonconsenting adult).*

The first thing that has to be done is to break the silence. This is the only way you can be sure that the abuse will stop. Though it may *seem* impossible to get up the nerve to tell someone, you *have* to do it.

# Who to Tell

If you have experienced abuse, it's critical that you tell someone—someone you can trust completely. Even so, it's possible that the first person you tell may not believe you. That's because people sometimes don't want to accept difficult news, so it's easier to believe it's not true. At this point it might be tempting to second-guess yourself or rationalize the situation: *I guess it wasn't really that bad. He probably didn't realize what he was doing.* Don't let yourself fall into that trap. What happened *really did* occur, and it was NOT right! You've been violated.

If the person you choose to tell doesn't believe you or doesn't do anything to help, find someone else to tell. Sexual abuse is complicated; you'll never be able to predict how another person will react to your news. But you *do* need to find a trusted adult who will believe you and believe *in* you.

But the question still remains, who should you tell? Here are some ideas:

• *Your mother.* If you've been abused by someone in your family, it's natural that you'd want your mom to know. She will be able to help stop the abusive situation and help you. Understand, though, that sometimes a mother has a *sense* that abuse is occurring but is incapable or unwilling to accept it. This might be because she too was a victim of incest, or perhaps because she's in denial (it's too painful for her to face the situation and do something about it, so she has convinced herself nothing is going on).

• *Your dad.* If your dad is not the abuser, it's likely that the abuse happened when he was away from home. He probably has no idea that you've been a victim. If your folks are separated or divorced, and you're living with your dad, he probably doesn't have a clue about what goes on in the other home where you stay.

Telling your dad may bring immediate results. He may react protectively and make sure the abuse stops right away. Still, it's possible that he will deny that anything has happened at all. If the abuse is coming from his side of the family (your uncle, grandfather, etc.), it may be difficult for him to perceive a close family member as a perpetrator (the one who commits the crime). Again, you can't predict how your father will react, but if you have a good relationship with him, you should confide in him and seek his help.

• *Other adults.* Only YOU have the power to break the silent trap you're in. If your mom or dad don't react positively and do something to help change your environment, tell another trusted adult. The important thing is not how many people you tell, but that you keep telling someone until the abuse stops. Here are a few other adults you might want to consider talking with:

• *Your teacher.* If you're too uncomfortable initiating a conversation like this with one of your favorite teachers, think about writing a note. Contrary to what many students think, most teachers really care about their students and will go the extra mile in offering help and guidance.

• *Your school counselor.* You might think the only thing they do is arrange and rearrange student schedules, but your school counselor has a degree in counseling and is prepared and equipped to help.

• *Your pastor, Sunday school teacher, or youth leader.* These people are in the positions they're in because they care about people and their needs. Consider asking one of these people if you can make an appointment with them to talk, or if the two of you can grab a Coke together. Being in a nonthreatening environment may help you to break the silence.

• *The Department of Social Services (DSS).*
It might be easier for you to talk with someone
you don't know. If this is the case, think about
calling a social worker or someone from the
social services agency in your area (check your
phone book or call information). These people
receive hundreds of calls and would more than
welcome yours! It might also be comforting to
know that they help thousands of teens—just
like you—in the same situation. They are
experts in handling domestic problems.

Let me be clear about what will happen if
DSS gets involved. If you talk to a social worker
or another representative at the Department of
Social Services and he or she determines that
you (or your friend) are in danger, you will
probably be removed from your home, at least
temporarily. A social worker's number-one job
is to protect you. You will most likely be sent to
a foster home for a short time. This will be difficult, there's no doubt about it. But don't let
your fear stop you from getting help. This is a
chance to break to the cycle of abuse once and
for all.

# Taking Care of YOU

Adults who commit incest often believe
they have power over the victim. In other
words, they're physically or emotionally
stronger than the young person they're abusing.

They have convinced themselves that they can make the victim keep silent and go along with the inappropriate behavior. And when a victim is much younger and physically weaker than the abuser, it may seem as though there's no other choice.

The abuser may threaten to harm the victim or other members of the victim's family if she tells. But the truth is, the abuser is committing a crime and should be stopped! If threats are made against you or someone you love, you need to take them seriously—but, if at all possible, don't let them keep you from speaking out and stopping the abuse.

YOU are the only one in the world who has the right to say who will touch your body. YOU'RE in charge of YOU. By saying (or screaming) no to the abuser, you're letting him know that your body is *not* up for grabs. You're also letting him know that you're aware that what he wants to do is wrong.

The moment a relative suggests something that makes you feel uncomfortable or touches you in a way that makes you uneasy, tell someone. By saying no to him and by telling someone else, you're putting an end to something before it even begins.

If you're alone in a room with someone who makes you feel uneasy, leave the room immediately. Don't worry about manners or appearing rude. It's much better to be impolite than to be abused!

## And If He's in the House . . .

If you're alone in your house with the abuser, here are a few things you can do to protect yourself:

• *Go to a friend's house.* The BEST alternative would be to leave the dangerous situation altogether. If you *can*, get out of your house and stay with a friend until the rest of your family is home.

• *Invite friends over to your house.* By having others around, you lessen the chances of abuse happening.

• *Don't take a bath or shower.* This would be putting yourself in an extremely vulnerable position. If you *have* to shower, make sure you lock the door, and ask a friend to call you back in 10 minutes to check on you.

• *Put a lock on your bedroom door.* If this is impossible, push furniture against your door at night. This way, the abuser will have to make a lot of noise when trying to enter your room, and that will alert the rest of the family.

## The Mailbag

Here are some of the questions I've received regarding sexual abuse. If someone you know is being sexually abused, maybe you can help them with these answers.

**Dear Susie:**

I'm 15, and my dad started sexually abusing me when I was eight years old. Last year I told my mom, and he's now going to counseling. The abuse has stopped, but I'm so confused about him. Even though he abused me, I still love him. At the same time, though, I hate him for what he did to me. Why am I so mixed up?

I'm so glad you told your mom! And I'm glad your dad is getting the help he needs. It sounds like you have a lot of courage. The confusion you're experiencing is normal. You want to love your dad because he's your dad. Every girl dreams of a father who will hold her, love her, and admire her. Even though your dad's love for you was twisted, it was still the only love you knew from him. So it's understandable why you still feel connected to him.

Instead of hating *him,* try to hate what he *did.* Sounds easy, but it's not. The only way you can accomplish this is with time, professional counseling, and especially God's help. But the exciting part is that you WANT to get past the hurt. That's the biggest step—and you've already taken it! Talk to your mom about finding a counselor in your area who can help you work through the confusion of your love/hate relationship with your dad.

Dear Susie:

My friend told me that her dad used to touch her in private places. Her parents are divorced now, and she never sees him anymore. I'm glad she trusted me enough to tell me that, but here's the part that confuses me. She said that even though she was really scared, she sort of enjoyed it. I don't get it. Is she crazy?

No, she's not crazy. And I'm glad the abuse isn't happening any longer. I'm also glad she has you for a friend. The fact that she trusts you shows you're capable of helping someone carry their problems.

God created us to desire intimacy with the opposite sex. And within the bonds of a lifetime marriage, sex can be the most wonderful gift in the world.

When she says she "sort of enjoyed it," she's talking about being sexually stimulated. Again, God created us to enjoy sex. It's normal for a girl to want to be close to a man, but your friend's father was committing a crime by touching her in private places and sexually stimulating her.

Although she didn't enjoy being *abused,* she enjoyed some of the feelings she received by being touched in a sensitive area. Many victims would agree with what she has said. The sad part is that many girls feel guilty for any feelings of pleasure the abuse may have produced.

Here's what your friend needs to understand: The feelings are normal. Her body was simply responding to sexual stimuli (and that's the way God created us). But she shouldn't feel guilty, because she is not to blame! She was abused. And that is *never* the fault of the victim.

**Dear Susie:**

**One of my male teachers puts his hand on the back of my neck and strokes me. It makes me nervous and uncomfortable. It happens when he's walking around the room. Like we'll all be taking a test, and he'll walk the aisles. Sometimes he stops at my desk and just does this. Am I paranoid?**

No, you're not paranoid. Your teacher has crossed a line, and chances are if he's doing this to you, he's probably doing it to other girls as well. It could be that he doesn't realize what he's doing. Some people are just touchy people. They hug a lot, give pats on the back, and squeeze shoulders. If he's doing this to girls *and* guys, he may be one of these people. But he still shouldn't be touching female students on the neck.

I suggest you talk to your parents about it. They might be willing to call him and inform him that this is not acceptable. If you feel you can handle confronting him, tell your parents you'd like to talk with him yourself. Before or after school, simply tell him that you're not comfortable with him touching you.

If the touching continues, ask your parents to make an appointment with the school administration.

**Dear Susie:**

**My parents were gone, and my boyfriend came over to study. We'd been sitting on the couch for about 30 minutes when he said he was hungry. I told him to go into the kitchen and help himself. He came back with a frozen hot dog and jammed it up me. I started crying and begged him to stop. He left angry. I feel so guilty. Why did he do this? I haven't told anyone, but I can't quit thinking about it. Please help me!**

I am so sorry! Your boyfriend committed a crime. He sexually molested you with an object. This is against the law! Let me suggest the following:

• Tell your parents. They need to know, and you need their support.

• Break up immediately! You deserve better. This guy obviously doesn't care about you. He needs professional help.

• With your parents' help, create some specific guidelines for your future dating relationships. Begin with vowing *never* to spend time with a guy alone in your house. Why? Because when no one's around, the temptation is too great to do something that probably wouldn't happen if parents were present.

• Talk with a counselor who can help you realize that this was NOT your fault. Don't blame yourself. You had no clue this was about to happen. There's no way you could have guessed what was going through your boyfriend's mind.

Why did he do this? It's my guess that he's been looking at some pornographic materials. Ever heard the phrase "garbage in = garbage out"? It's true. We have to be very selective about what we read, watch, and listen to, because what we pour into our minds will eventually seep out in our lives.

**Dear Susie:**
**Everyone says you should tell if you're being abused. But my friend says she won't tell because she's afraid her parents will get divorced, and then it will be all her fault. What really happens when you tell?**

Holding her family together is not her responsibility. That's a choice her parents have to make, and she shouldn't base her decision on what might or might not happen.

If your friend tells a school counselor, the counselor is required by law to contact the Department of Social Services. Sometimes the victim is temporarily removed from the home (and placed in a foster home, with extended family members, or with a close friend) while the abuser gets help. And sometimes the abuser is temporarily removed from the home.

Yes, sometimes families split. But your friend needs to realize that the trouble in her parents' marriage started long before her abuse.

It's certainly understandable to be frightened of having to leave your home—after all, that's her only security—even though it's a dysfunctional sense of security. And as an abused child, she desperately wants to hold the fragmented pieces of her family together. So why should she tell if she might have to leave home or risk tearing her family apart?

• Because if she doesn't, the abuse will continue and she may end up pregnant.

• Because she deserves much better.

• Because she needs to learn the difference between real love and false love.

• Because the longer she waits, the harder it will be to put a stop to the dysfunction, and she may end up marrying an abuser or becoming an abuser since that's all she will have known.

• Because she has the right to control her own body.

• Because God desires a better life for her.

**Dear Susie:**
    **I was sexually abused a couple of years ago, and I think I've worked through it. But**

now I'm starting to date, and when a guy starts getting physical with me, I find that it's hard to say no.

The guy I'm dating lies on top of me and kinda moves around. I really don't want him to do that, but why can't I tell him not to?

Sounds like you're having trouble knowing what the boundaries are in a normal guy-girl relationship. Even though you *think* you've worked through your past abuse, there are still some things you need to sort through.

You're probably having trouble telling him no because when you were a victim, the abuser had power over you. In other words, he may have physically forced himself on you. Since you had to cooperate then, you feel you have to cooperate now. In a sense, you feel powerless to set limits. But a dating situation isn't an abusive situation (unless it's date rape). I'm assuming the guys you go out with are people you've already established a friendship with.

If you're old enough to handle the responsibility of dating, then you're old enough to declare your boundaries—and yes, he's gone too far!

I suggest you sit down with your parents or youth leader and talk specifically about how to establish healthy, godly dating relationships. For more information, you can purchase these books: *What Hollywood Won't Tell You About Sex, Love and Dating* by Greg Johnson and Susie Shellenberger

(Regal Books) and *Anybody Got a Clue About Guys?* by Susie Shellenberger (Servant Publishers).

## What's Really Important

We've looked at a lot of information about sexual abuse, but there are two things I want you to remember above all else:

1. It was NOT your fault!
2. Tell a trusted adult (or adults).

Now let's move on to Part III, which presents two fiction stories about teen girls who are forced to face abuse in their lives.

# Part III

## Fiction

# Silent Haunting

*Pat's vacation turned into her worst nightmare. She just couldn't bear the ugly memory any longer. . . .*

by Lonnie Collins Pratt

Pat sat huddled among the lakefront brush, burrowing into the sand dunes, her knees drawn up beneath her chin, her eyes fixed distantly, while she held herself tightly to keep from coming apart. She wished the nauseous feeling would go away.

Someone would find out. And if someone found out, she would die. She clenched her eyes and drew in a long, ragged breath, trying to reassure herself that no one had to find out. She could keep this secret.

But something was wrong inside of her, with the way she acted and looked and talked. She knew when she looked in the mirror that morning something was different from before. It jumped out at her. How would she get through the rest of vacation without someone seeing it too? How would she face people again? Pat decided she wouldn't.

She'd stay out on the beach and die alone. Alone with the memory of last night, the feel of cold hands on her and the darkness of his laugh. He had forced on her the secret of who he was, of his twisted way.

She hated him so completely that it made her weak attempting to control and cope with the fury of her feelings. He would enjoy flaunting it in front of everyone. He would visit the campgrounds, smile and talk with her parents like a normal nephew and cousin. She could see his leering smile and eyes daring her to tell them, knowing she had crippled that part of her that could trust enough to tell.

She could *never* tell. She'd shrink, run, hide. It was settled then. She just couldn't return to the campsite. She couldn't return to her mother and father. She couldn't be their bubbly, fun-loving Patty again. Nothing would ever be the same again.

She wished he were dead. She wished it with all her strength and might. *Die, die, die,* she thought. But she couldn't will him into death or disappearance. She couldn't wish away last night.

## The Secret Revealed

She knew a lot of time had passed, and her family would be looking for her. She had gone from her aunt's house to the beach, never returning to the trailer. The thought of living with this all day was impossible. Tomorrow was unbearable. Better there be no tomorrow, no today. Everyone would blame her. They'd know she was bad, used, dirty.

She heard her cousin Debbie calling her name over and over, but she didn't answer. Debbie was *his* sister.

Pat sat perfectly still, praying she'd shut up and go away. The voice grew louder, nearer. *I should run,* Pat thought. *Or hide. Maybe I should just hide. I can't let her find me.*

It was too late. Debbie walked into the small clearing, put her hands on her hips, and looked at Pat. "What are you doing? Everyone is frantic."

Pat looked out at the lake. It seemed soothing—the water, the sky, the silence.

"Are you all right, Patty?"

Debbie walked like him, her hair was the

same sandy brown, her skin the same freckled, sunburned pink. *Go away, Debbie. Please go away,* Pat begged silently.

Debbie sat down beside her. "What's wrong?"

"Nothing," Patty snapped. "Leave me alone."

"It's a nice spot, but you should have told your mother you were going off to daydream. They're worried."

Debbie looked curiously at Patty, then put her hand on her shoulder. "You're not fine at all."

"I asked you to leave!" Patty blasted. "Doesn't anyone in your family respect others' rights?"

"Who are you mad at? Did you have a major battle with someone? My brother, maybe?"

Pat wanted to sink into the sand and never come out. The thought of him was so over-whelming it seemed to drip over her like heavy slime, completely covering her.

Debbie studied Pat's red, swollen eyes, her pale complexion, and the trembling bottom lip. She knew that haunted, suffering look in her young cousin's eyes. "No . . . not again . . . I'm sorry, Patty," she whispered.

The horrified tone of Debbie's words fright-ened Pat. Their eyes met for the first time. Debbie, 18 years old, had just graduated from high school. Her whole life was new and fresh before her. Lucky Debbie.

Debbie's fingers gripped the younger girl's chin. "Tell me the truth. What happened? What did he do to you?"

*She only had to look at me and she saw it,* Pat thought. She bolted to her feet and raced toward the water, away from the questions and the knowing gaze. The water would wash away the slime . . . the scars. The water would silence the memory forever.

## No Running Away

Debbie was on her heels. She gripped Pat's arms and spun her around. "You have to tell me," she ordered desperately, her voice shaking.

Pat hated the touch of hands. Violently, she threw her arms down, knocking Debbie's hands away. "Don't! Don't touch me! Not ever!"

She felt caged, surrounded with nowhere to run. The water seemed to call her, inviting her to end her torture.

"Okay, I won't touch you. Please listen. Don't run. You don't have to talk. Just listen."

Pat pushed the blonde hair off her forehead and shut her eyes. Maybe if she listened, Debbie would leave. Pat nodded.

"I understand. You think no one can, but I do. I was 12, a year younger than you, when he first came into my room in the middle of the night," Debbie said. "It still haunts me. I know, believe me, I do. I never told my parents. He said he'd tell them that I asked him to do it. I was so scared, like you are. I felt dirty and ashamed. He's my brother! Doesn't he know brothers aren't supposed to touch their own sisters?

"I didn't think it involved anyone else. He left home. The torment doesn't stop when he leaves. It won't stop when you go home. Not unless you stop it by telling someone."

Tears streamed down Debbie's perfectly made-up face. "Let's put an end to his power to hurt us—let's tell someone. Don't you see? If we say nothing, it'll happen again. It could be your little sister or someday your daughter . . . or mine. It won't stop if he can humiliate us into silence."

"No!" Pat screamed, choking on her tears. She turned and ran toward the water screaming, "I can't! I couldn't stand anyone knowing he touched me! I couldn't!"

Debbie grabbed her tightly, forcing her to stop running. She stood in her path. "Please, I need you to come with me. He can't claim we're lying if we're together."

"He will. He'll say that I asked for it, that I wanted him to touch me. He said he would!"

"We'll make our parents believe the truth. They love us. You don't want to live with this alone. I've done it, and it only gets worse."

Pat's eyes flew open, and a sob caught her breath as she tried to speak. "It couldn't get worse. I'll die if it gets worse." She covered her mouth, feeling as if she'd throw up. She couldn't think anymore. She had to find a way to erase last night—fling it into nonexistence.

Debbie moved tentatively toward Pat. "We'll beat him if we tell. I know you're afraid and you're ashamed of what happened. You think they'll blame you. I've felt that for six years. But seeing you—a kid—so scared and violated. . . . It isn't your fault, Patty. And it isn't mine. It's his. His sickness. His ugliness. We can't let him go on hurting people. Help me stop him, Patty. Otherwise, we'll both be in the room with him next time he prowls in the dark."

*Next time,* Pat thought. *How many next times had there been for Debbie? How many days, months, years of living with this black, silent haunting? Next time?!*

Pat couldn't endure a next time. She couldn't let it happen again—to anyone.

Slowly, Debbie extended her hand to Pat. *Trust, touch, help me,* Debbie's eyes begged. Pat took hold of her cousin's hand. Together they would make sure no one had to live with a next time. ■

*Lonnie Collins Pratt lives in Ann Arbor, Mich., and works for Servant Publications.*

# The Secret

*Many girls are abused, harassed, or victimized by someone outside the family. You may have a friend who's been raped, fondled, or molested by a stranger, a date, a teacher, or even a leader in her church. Sexual abuse—regardless of who commits it—is always traumatic.*

*This fiction story deals with abuse involving someone outside the family.*

by Barbara Santucci

W hy are you angry, Kim?" Mom asked. "If you don't want to go to the movies with Dad and me, that's fine."

"Sorry, Mom." I pulled my books out of my backpack and set them on my desk. "I have a lot of homework to do this weekend."

"Is everything all right? You seem upset lately." Mom brushed my bangs off my forehead.

"Everything's fine. I'm just tired." I turned my head away so she couldn't look me in the eyes. Mom could always tell when I was lying.

She shoved aside the dirty clothes on my bed and sat down. "Maybe keeping up with school and trying out for the basketball team is putting too much pressure on you." Mom stared at me. It felt as if she had X-ray vision and could see right through me.

"I'm okay, really," I lied. "You and Dad have fun."

"Why don't you invite Michelle over? Maybe she could spend the night."

"Sure." But I knew I wouldn't. These past two weeks I just wanted to be alone; that way, there was less chance of blurting out the secret, especially to my best friend.

When Mom finally left my room, I decided to take a shower—my third of the day. I took a lot of showers lately—I never felt clean. I scrubbed and scrubbed until my skin felt raw. Then the tears began.

*I feel dirty, Lord. I can't scrub away the memory of Coach Greene's hands. They were all over me after practice today.*

It all began two weeks ago when Coach Greene said to me, "Kim, can you stay after a few minutes?"

"Sure thing, Coach." I sat on a bench and waited until the gym cleared out.

"Kim, you want to be on the team, right?"

I nodded.

"Well," he continued as he sat down next to me, "you're one of the tallest girls trying out, and I'd like you to play center. But your shooting skills are weak. Are you willing to put in extra practice time?"

"Sure!"

"Let's start right now. First, let me give you a few pointers."

I jumped up, and we began a game of one-on-one. After a while, Coach Greene started to guard me a little too closely, and I was uncomfortable. I thought I felt his hands on my back, but I decided it must be my imagination.

When we finished, he said, "Kim, I like you a lot, and I want you on my team. Let's work on your shooting next time."

"That would be great," I said, staring at his basketball shoes. But an uneasiness seeped into me. "Bye, Coach Greene."

The next day after practice, the coach and I worked on free-throw shots. He came up behind me to demonstrate and pressed his body into mine. With each shot, he continued to press against me. I felt his hand on my back, my side, then he put his hand on my breast. I froze.

Coach Greene moved away from me and acted as if nothing was wrong. "Final cuts are next week. I'd sure like to put your name on the list. Keep up the good work."

My head felt like it was in a fog. Had I imagined what happened? Was I going crazy? "I—I've got to go," I stammered as I escaped from the gym. I didn't stop running until I reached the front door of my house.

I was glad Mom and Dad weren't home. I went straight to the bathroom and into the shower. I felt numb as the water beat down on me. That was the day the showers began. First one, then two, then sometimes three each evening after practice.

## Bittersweet Moment

A week later, the list for the high school team was posted outside the gym.

"Look!" screamed Michelle. "We made it, Kim!"

I started to jump up and down with Michelle. For a few moments, I was really excited, but not for long.

Reality came crashing down. Everything had changed. Basketball wasn't fun anymore, and I didn't feel a part of this team. I felt different. Dirty.

I tried to stay caught up in the excitement around me, the hugs, screams, jumps for joy.

"Now you can relax a little, Kimmy," Michelle said. "You've been so wired these past two weeks. Let's go to a movie this weekend and celebrate."

"Sure." I put on a false smile.

After school, the new team met in the gym. "Congratulations, team players," shouted Coach Greene. "You can pick up your uniforms after practice. Now let's get to work."

That night after practice, Coach Greene told me to stay after a few minutes because he had something to discuss with me. When everyone had cleared out of the gym, he stepped so close to me that his words felt like slaps on my face. "Kim, if you tell anybody about our little friendship, I'll say my only interest in you is to develop you into a good center for the team." He began to twirl a stray strand of my hair and pulled me close to him. "You know, girls your age often have crushes on their coaches. It's only normal." Then he kissed me on the lips.

I broke away from him and raced home, where I went straight into the shower. I tried to scrub away the memory of his smile, his voice, his eyes, his hands.

And I wondered if I'd made the team because of what Coach Greene called "our little friendship." Was I really any good?

# Self-Doubt Sets In

I decided to prove to myself that I deserved to be a team player by scoring the most points in the games. Every night I put on sweats and practiced shooting baskets in my driveway. I kept practicing until I could shoot well from the perimeter. When Coach Greene noticed my improvement, he called it determination—focus. Michelle called it an obsession.

"Lighten up, Kim," Michelle told me over the phone one Saturday morning. "Let's take a break and go to the mall. We can look at the spring clothes—"

"No," I interrupted. "I was just going outside to shoot some more baskets, then I have to work on my science project."

"Oh, Kim, chill out! You're already the highest scorer on the team, and those science projects aren't due for three weeks. Besides, you've lost a few pounds, and you'll look super in those new skirts that just came in at the Gap."

"I'll have to ask my mom. I'll call you back."

Suddenly, a voice came from the doorway. "Ask me what?" I hadn't seen my mom standing there. "May I come in?" she asked.

"Sure. Michelle asked me to go to the mall with her."

"Great idea. Perfect day for a time-out. You've been working hard lately. Dad and I have been worried about you."

I couldn't look at her. Tears threatened to spill over my face.

"You haven't spent much time with your friends lately."

"With homework, games, and practices, I guess there's not much free time."

"Why don't you go with Michelle? It would do you good."

"Let me decide what's good for me!" I snapped.

"What's wrong, Kim?" Mom came closer and held my face in her hands. "Can we talk about it?"

I wished I could, but where would I begin? Besides, I was so ashamed. What if I had done something to make Coach Greene think I liked his touches and kisses?

"Mom, there's nothing to talk about." I pulled away from her and started to walk out of my room. "I need to take a shower."

## The Truth

Tears poured down my face as the water rushed over my body. *Dear God, I miss my old life, when school was fun, being with my friends was fun, and basketball was fun.*

I turned off the shower and wrapped a towel around me before going into my room. I was startled to see my mom still sitting on my bed. Her face was all wrinkled up—like it always is when she's worried.

"Kim, look at you. You're skin and bones, you take three or four showers a day, and you're edgy all the time. I need to know what's wrong." Mom's voice started to tremble.

"There's nothing wrong, Mom. The only problem I have is a lack of privacy."

"Kim, Kim . . . " Mom started to cry as she walked over and wrapped her arms around me.

"Don't touch me!" I shouted. "Just get out!"

"I *won't* get out. I'm not leaving this room until you tell me what's happened to you. Nothing you've done could ever change how I feel about you."

Tears streamed down my face as I backed into a corner and fell in a heap on the floor.

Mom sat next to me and rocked me in her arms for the longest time as the whole horrible story about Coach Greene poured out.

"You didn't do anything wrong, Kim," said Mom, as she stroked my hair. "It was Coach Greene who did something wrong to you."

That afternoon, Mom and Dad called the principal and set up an appointment for Monday at 8:00 A.M. The thought of telling the truth about what happened between Coach Greene and me didn't make me very happy, but I was sure it was better than living alone with my secret.

I knew that Coach Greene would be

disciplined, maybe even fired. If I didn't tell the truth, he would have continued abusing me. He might even hurt other girls. I knew I was doing the right thing by speaking out, regardless of the consequences.

I prayed a lot that weekend as I thought over and over again about our meeting with the principal, and I held Psalm 34:5 close to my heart: "Those who look to him are radiant; their faces are never covered with shame" (NIV). ■

*Barbara Santucci lives in Rockford, Ill.*

*Part IV*

# Healing

# Jill's Story

*Jill works down the hall from me at Focus on the Family. She's an outgoing, beautiful young lady. You'd never guess that years of pain lie hidden behind her smile. Though she's never publicly shared the hurt she has experienced, she wants to offer hope to teen girls who may be trapped in incestuous homes. Therefore, she has decided to talk about her past right now. Here's her story.*

My parents divorced when I was only six months old. My mom abandoned me because I reminded her of my dad. She said I was a fat, ugly baby and didn't want anything to do with me. So I ended up at my grandmother's house—with my mom's mother. That's who raised me.

My grandmother was perfect on the outside. She and Grandpa had lots of money and could always afford the most fashionable clothes and the best of everything. We all went to church every Sunday, smiling on the outside but falling apart on the inside. You see, Grandma was mentally ill and emotionally abusive.

She constantly said hurtful things to me, such as, "We buy you such pretty clothes, but they look so horrible on you. Too bad you're not a pretty girl."

And she played weird mind games with me. For instance, she'd point to a red book and ask, "Jill, what color is that?"

"It's red, Grandma," I'd say.

Then she'd start screaming and violently insist that it was blue. She'd point her finger at me and yell, "You're an idiot, Jill! You're so stupid!" This would go on and on until I'd finally give in and agree that it was blue.

You can imagine after *years* of this, I began to see the world around me in her abnormal way. I learned not to trust what *I* perceived as reality, but to accept *her* reality instead. Soon I began believing that I really *was* fat, useless, and ugly.

Grandma was extremely controlling. She read all my letters and monitored all my phone calls. I had no privacy. My entire world revolved around whatever she wanted it to be.

## Feeling Trapped

When I was 13 years old, my grandpa died, and it seemed as though something snapped inside my grandmother, making her even crazier. Her brother—my great-uncle—began coming around. She said it was because Uncle Mac wanted to represent a father figure to me.

He started picking me up after school and taking me to movies and fancy, four-star restaurants. One evening as we walked to his car, he cornered me between another car and a wall. I was shocked when he slid his hand up my shorts. I pushed him away and screamed, "What are you doing?"

But he grabbed me and pushed me against the car, pressing his body close to mine and rubbing himself against me. I felt dirty and ashamed. I began thinking it was all my fault. *I shouldn't have worn these shorts,* I thought. *I'm so stupid! I must have given him some kind of signal or something.*

Even though I blamed myself for what had happened, I knew that what he had done was wrong. I'm not sure *how* I knew; I just knew it.

When I got home, Grandma was standing at the kitchen sink, washing dishes. I told her exactly what had happened. She was furious! She pulled a wet plate out of the sink and hurled it at me while screaming, "You're a liar! You're a no-good liar, Jill!"

Then she locked me in my bedroom for two days. The only time I was allowed to come out was to use the bathroom. I received no food and no water. She said I wouldn't be released from my room until I admitted that I had lied.

Finally, I couldn't stand being a prisoner in my bedroom any longer. I gave in just to be able to eat and get dressed and walk around the house. She then called Uncle Mac and told him to come over because I had something to tell him.

I was then forced to apologize for what I had said. I had to tell him that I lied, and I had to agree to continue seeing him.

## Other Problems

By the time I was in high school, I had developed bulimia, an eating disorder. Oftentimes, eating disorders can be traced to abuse. I realized that my great-uncle had sexually abused me, but I didn't realize that I was being emotionally abused by Grandma. She was constantly telling me I was fat, stupid, and worthless. I knew she was mentally ill, and it was obvious that she was mean and controlling, but I didn't know this was considered emotional abuse.

Controlling my food intake was one way that I could take charge. Subconsciously, I wanted to control my own life and my own body. No one else could dictate what I would eat or wouldn't eat. I wanted everything on the outside to look as perfect as possible in order to make up for how lousy I felt on the inside.

Right before my high school graduation, Grandma told me that she knew where my dad was. I hadn't been in contact with him at all, so you can imagine my surprise to learn his whereabouts! She allowed me to send him a graduation announcement. He attended the graduation and even treated me to dinner.

We really clicked. I loved being with him, and he seemed so sympathetic and understanding. He had learned—even through the short time he was married to my mom—what my grandma was like. I felt I had finally found an understanding friend. We promised to keep in touch after I got to college.

As I left for college, I was totally unprepared for living and relating in a normal world. It was hard for me to make good decisions. I had to depend a lot on what others told me, because I had spent years with an abusive relative pounding false reality into my brain.

I started dating a guy who was also emotionally abusive. Thinking back on it, maybe I was drawn to him because that's what I was used to. I found out later that he was a serial rapist on our campus. He stood in front of the dorms and studied the freshman girls going in and out. He watched them long enough that he could tell which ones struggled with low self-esteem. Naturally, I was an easy target.

He befriended me and started the relationship by showering me with kindness. But it wasn't too long before he began being extremely possessive. He isolated me until he was the only person I saw, and he began controlling my life. Again, since I was used to this from living with my grandma, it all seemed normal.

## Bad News

One night he called and canceled our date, so I went out to eat with a girlfriend. It just so happened that we spotted him at the same restaurant with another girl. I was furious! I told him I never wanted to see him again.

Later, he phoned me while drunk and began calling me every horrible name in the book. I held my ground, though, and said it was over. A couple of days passed, and he called again—asking if we could talk. I turned him down and repeated that we were finished.

A few hours later, I heard a knock on my door. I thought it was the girl down the hall returning some books I had loaned her. I opened the door and saw *him* instead.

He was extremely apologetic and nice, and even though I knew I shouldn't, I let him in. When he began talking about getting back together, I continued to stand my ground. "We can't," I said. "It's over. I don't want to go out with you anymore."

He became angry and started screaming at me, so I told him to leave. "Then open the door and let me out!" he yelled.

I stepped past him to turn the doorknob, but as I did, he grabbed me from behind. He threw me down and raped me. I screamed, but no one could hear because he held a pillow over my face.

I reported it to the campus police, and they questioned him, but he had made up an alibi. He had some friends say that he was in his room the entire time.

Two days later, as I was coming out of a night class, he jumped out of the bushes and beat me up. He tore a muscle in my back and dislocated my vertebrae. I was in a wheelchair for six weeks.

"If you don't drop the charges," he threatened, "I'll kill you."

I knew he meant business, and I was scared to death! He began stalking me—no matter what time it was or where I was, he was there. After several weeks, I was such an emotional wreck that I dropped the charges.

## A Downward Spiral

When I went back to Grandma's house in June, I was really restless. I had tasted freedom while away at college, and I didn't like being in her emotionally unstable and controlling environment any longer. I was also still trying to get over the rape, and I just needed a friend.

A college pal who lived a couple of hours away invited me to come spend a week with her family. Grandma said I could go, and I excitedly packed enough clothes for seven days. *This is exactly what I need,* I thought. Then for some unknown reason, on the day I was supposed to leave, Grandma changed her mind.

"If you leave for a week, I'll make sure you leave for good!" she snarled. She started throwing my belongings everywhere. I was so tired of all the violence in my life that I decided to go ahead and leave, even though I knew I would never have a home with her again.

I ended up coming back in two days, and my room was totally empty. All my possessions were gone! It was as if I had never existed. I told Dad what was going on, and he invited me to come stay with him and his wife.

Two weeks after I moved in with Dad, he started molesting me. It started with simple touching. He began touching me underneath my nightgown while saying, "You have nowhere else to go. I'm all you have. Just relax and go along with this, or you'll have nothing!" The abuse progressed from his touching me to him forcing me to touch him. From there, the abuse got worse and worse, until finally, he started having intercourse with me.

Eventually, I moved out of my dad's house, putting an end to the abuse, and finished my college degree. Breaking out of the abusive situation was the first step toward healing.

## Putting the Pieces Back Together

The hopeful news I want to share with you is that you—or the friend you're seeking to help—can overcome an abusive background and find healing and wholeness.

All my life, I continued going to church, reading my Bible, and depending on God's guidance to get me through the traumatic times. And you know? Even though life wasn't fair, God was always there. He provided the strength I needed to carry on despite the abuse, and He walked with me through the nightmares.

I began going to counseling a year ago, and I'm getting stronger every day. God is helping me heal, and I now know He can make something beautiful out of *anything!* Through counseling and with God's help, I'm putting myself back together again. I'm slowly learning that I can trust my own view of reality. I'm becoming one person—whole and free! The path to healing has, indeed, been long and difficult. But the good news is that there's hope for anyone who has been abused.

Counseling is often hard work. It's not easy to talk about the pain and hard times I've experienced. But healing is so important to me that sharing the hurt is worth it. There's no way I could do this without God. He gives me hope and fills my life with purpose and meaning.

I'm now 33 years old, and God has blessed me with a terrific Christian husband and two great children. It's taken a while, but I've finally learned that my self-worth doesn't come from what other people say about me. For years I thought I was no good because the people closest to me kept telling me how rotten I was.

I now know that my self-image comes from being unconditionally loved and totally accepted by God. Can you imagine how free that makes me feel? I don't have to live in the past anymore! I don't have to dwell on trying to understand *why* this or that happened. I can simply relax and bask in His great, overflowing love for me.

What about you? Do you have a friend who has been abused? Have *you* experienced incest? Though it may seem impossible, I want you to know that you CAN get your life back! You CAN become the young lady God intends for you to be. Please believe me—there IS life after abuse.

⌒⌒

*If you're in an abusive situation, your head is probably spinning right now. You want help putting the pieces of your life back together, but at the same time, you need a little guidance on where to begin.*

*Though this is a problem that can't be solved overnight, let me be your big sis for a few minutes and walk through a game plan with you, okay?*

**1. Strengthen your spiritual life.** There's absolutely no way you can fight this battle alone. You need God's help. Ask Him to strengthen you and give you wisdom—then do *your* part: Read your Bible every day and talk to Him. You see, God isn't a big, cosmic creator hiding somewhere up in the clouds. He's your best friend (or He *wants* to be, if you'll let Him), and just like any friendship, good communication is essential. So talk to Him. He feels your pain *with* you.

Ask God to help you get to the point of telling an adult. The wonderful thing about our God is that He'll never force us into doing anything. But He *will* gently guide. If you don't *want* to tell anyone, tell Him that; then ask Him to help you *want to want* to tell someone.

**2. Find a skilled counselor.** The benefit of talking with a professional counselor is that he or she has dealt with this problem before. A counselor can help you sort out your feelings and help you understand yourself and your family. Most important, counseling will help you move forward and find emotional healing.

**3. Rebuild your trust in yourself and other people.** If you've been abused, it's understandable why it's hard for you to trust people. But the fact is there are hundreds of people in your immediate world who *are* trustworthy and who *do* want to help. Seek these people out and strive to establish close friendships.

**4. Don't bury your pain.** Though you may *want* to keep shoving your terrible secret deeper and deeper inside your heart, it needs to come out. Think of your emotional pain as a physical wound. If you fell down and scraped your knee, we'd put a Band-Aid on it. But sooner or later, we'd need to take the Band-Aid off and let your wound get some air. Why? Because that's essential for complete healing to take place.

It works the same way with emotional pain. You may *want* to keep putting Band-Aids on it and keep covering it up, but for healing to take place, you eventually have to air the pain.

Strive to work through the hurt. Begin keeping a journal. Record your feelings and why you're hurting. If something happens at school that triggers a bad memory or a painful moment, write it down.

# With God, Nothing Is Hopeless

I hope by the time you're finished with this book, you'll have gained some hope. No matter how bad your nightmare is, it's not hopeless. Try to think of these pages as a big hug. The people who put this book together care about you. And the people in your church, your town, and your school care about you. Most important, God cares about you—big time! Though you may *feel* completely alone, you are NOT.

Never in a million years would Jill have dreamed that she would have such a wonderful husband and children, a loving church family, and a job that she's crazy about. God is faithful. He knows your hurt. And He wants to begin the healing process in you . . . right now.

Repeat after me: "God loves me right now just as I am—not as I *should* be." Let's repeat it again: "God loves me right now just as I am—not as I should be."

Do yourself a favor. Memorize that. Then ask Him to start putting the broken pieces of your life back together again. In Him, there IS wholeness.

Need to talk? Give one of our counselors a call (phone number below). We're here for you.

## Help is Available

Your local phone book will have several hot line numbers listed on the inside front cover. Consider calling one of those numbers or one of the following:

- Abuse Registry  1-800-962-2873
- Child Abuse/Family Violence 1-800-422-4453
- Focus on the Family  (ask for the counseling department) 1-800-232-6459
- Minirth Meier New Life Clinics 1-800-NEW-HOPE